7 Keys to Prophetic Protocol

Protocol

The Practice of the Prophetic Volume 2

SAMUEL MEDINA

ACKNOWLEDGMENTS

Over the past year since I wrote the first book in this series, *7 Keys to Prophetic Maturity*, I've been amazed at the response I received from God's people around the world, and so first I want to express my gratitude toward God for seeing fit to use me to benefit his people. I'm also grateful for my wife, whose support and prayer have been vital to my writing, and whose editorial input has been invaluable.

To everyone who has been a part of the process of the production and promotion of this book, I am forever grateful, and pray God's blessing on your lives.

In His service,

Sam

DEDICATION

To Jesus Christ, the author and finisher of our faith. Lord, come quickly.

Books by Sam Medina

The Hot Cold Call

Katarina the Dragonslayer and the Foebreaker's Curse

Apostolic Foundations: Eternal Principles for God-ordained Christian Leadership

Fitness for Spiritual Warfare

7 Keys to Prophetic Maturity

CONTENTS

Foreword

The prophet can be said to have many functions, including but not limited to prophesying, intercession, giving counsel, or even governing a nation, but if we are to gain a basic understanding of the underlying principles of prophetic protocol there is one truth that must first be grasped. The entirety of the prophet's purpose will always center around two things: *perception* and *disclosure*.

Indeed, all of the failings which occur in the execution prophetic ministry have to do with one or both of these two things. Sometimes at the heart of the problem is a lack of maturity on the part of the prophet, or even presumption, but regardless of the causality of a prophetic misstep, mistakes of any sort in the perceiving or disclosure of prophetic revelation can be dangerous, even disastrous for believers, especially if they are new to the faith or weak in it.

Over the last sixteen years in my study of scripture and in executing prophetic ministry I have observed that there is a definitive protocol that, when followed, will prevent errors both in perception and disclosure. In some cases, these were things which the Lord showed me during times of consecration and study, or which He brought to my attention when I observed erroneous prophecies, or when the Lord stopped me before I put my foot in my mouth.

Doubtless there are those who may make the claim that they are led by the spirit, and therefore don't need any rules to work by, but most of the time such assertions are an indicator that the opposite is true, because the fruit of the Holy Spirit includes **discipline**.

For the purposes of this book, when the term 'church' is used, it can be applied to any fellowship of believers in Jesus Christ, whether large or small, including house churches and other gatherings of the saints.

This having been said, it is my earnest hope and prayer, that this simple approach will deepen your understanding of the prophetic, and help you to administer your gifting with grace and clarity.

1
CERTAINTY OF REVELATION

Beloved, do not believe every spirit, but test the spirits, whether they are of God; because many false prophets have gone out into the world. By this you know the Spirit of God: Every spirit that confesses that Jesus Christ has come in the flesh is of God, and every spirit that does not confess that Jesus Christ has come in the flesh is not of God. And this is the spirit of the Antichrist, which you have heard was coming, and is now already in the world. You are of God, little children, and have overcome them, because He who is in you is greater than he who is in the world. They are of the world. Therefore they speak as of the world, and the world hears them. We are of God. He who knows God hears us; he who is not of God does not hear us. By this we know the spirit of truth and the spirit of error. (1 John 4:6)

Now, there are probably many people out there who serve in prophetic ministry who wouldn't think of this as part of protocol. There are even others who teach young prophets to approach prophecy as if it were guesswork. One pastor I knew years ago went so far as to say, "You learn prophecy by trial and error." Not only is this wrong, it's tremendously dangerous.

Let's think for a moment. If you needed to install new brakes on your car, would you bring it to a mechanic who didn't even know what size discs and rotors to use? Would you let him work on your car if he said, "Well, these rotors might be too big and cause your brakes to fail, but I do this by trial and error, so don't worry about it." How much confidence would he inspire? If you needed brain surgery, would you accept the services of a surgeon who told you he was going to operate by trail and error?

Now, these examples might seem absurd, and they are intended to seem that way. No one in their right mind would use that mechanic or surgeon. We would probably all agree that our relationship with God is more important than our physical safety and well-being. Yet so many of us have been taught to accept that prophecy ought to involve guesswork, or that it's a matter of trial and error. Such attitudes inevitably lead to problems, up to and including demonic infiltration. How do we know this?

If you have to TRY, God isn't in it.

First, there was never so much as one prophet in the Bible who was in right standing with God who ever needed to guess. Elijah never said, "I think God might have said that it's not going to rain for a while." Some may argue that we're under the New Testament, and that there is grace, but the truth is that the New Testament is a **better** covenant. Grace does not lower the standard, but rather empowers the believer to achieve the standard. If you don't believe this, no New Testament prophet in the Bible ever had to guess, either.

There are several dangers in guessing, or just running with a prophecy we're unsure of. First, we can be **wrong**, and thereby mislead people into acting on a word that wasn't even from God in the first place. There are already far too many people shipwrecked in their faith because they thought the prophet had really heard from God, acted on what they were told, and disaster ensued.

Another danger that arises from the 'trial and error' approach is that of infiltration by a spirit of error. In the New Testament, we are shown that the opposite of the Spirit of Truth is the spirit of error. Thus, if we approach prophecy as a matter of trial and error, we can very well be unwittingly submitting our gift to the spirit of error.

Now, some leaders who teach on prophecy will argue against this. They will usually make use of such witty expressions like "You can't throw the baby out with the bath water." Often this expression is used even when defending the clearly erroneous prophecies of high-profile prophets who've been in ministry for decades. When you've been in ministry for that long, you ought to know the voice of God, and no matter how long you have ministered in the prophetic, if you're not absolutely certain you've heard from God, it's best to keep quiet. This of course will bring up the question of emerging prophets and whether they ought to be given the freedom to 'test' their gift in a 'safe' environment.

The training of an emerging prophet ought to include development of character, and the testing of his prophecies, but it is best that such things not be done around the general congregation. It is also important to note that this emerging tradition of making young prophets 'practice' prophesying is simply not scriptural, nor is it healthy for the prophet or those to whom he is ministering.

First, it teaches the young prophet the habit of **trying** to prophesy. We've already established that no Biblical prophet ever had to **try**. God either spoke to him, or He didn't. There is such a thing as inquiring of the Lord, as prophets in Biblical times did, but there should never be such as thing as **trying** to prophesy. This kind of pressure to perform is at best detrimental to developing the habit of trusting God to speak or be silent according to **His** will, ad at worst it is conducive to spirits of divination, which have become common in prophetic ministry.

In recent years I've seen some leaders start to incorporate New Age practices into prophetic ministry. Some of these include transcendental meditation, attempts at remote viewing, and trying to 'work up' prophecy based on common objects or even pictures. Some will even tell prophets they need to 'step out in faith' to prophesy. Such a notion is absurd. Either God has revealed something to you, or he hasn't. None of these methods are necessary, and all of them bring with them the very real danger of demonic influence and infiltration.

Yes, we ought to meditate on the Word of God, but Scripture never tells us to clear our minds or to 'soak' in music whose origins are in Eastern mysticism. It's good to worship, but beware of transcendental meditation disguised as worship! If a prophet tells you to clear your mind, **get out of that place immediately**! This something occultists do to render people more susceptible to hypnotic suggestion, and it also can make one susceptible to demonic infiltration. This brings us to our next point.

A real prophecy, and a real prophet can stand to be tested.

Some very popular prophets now tell their audiences, 'Don't test the spirits. Just trust us. In the end, you'll see that we were right." If you hear a prophet say something like this, stay away from them. We are told repeatedly throughout Scripture to test and judge prophecy (1 John 4:1, 1 Thessalonians 5:20-21, e.g.). We'll deal more fully with the issue of just how to test prophecy, in Chapter 7, but for we can at least say that genuine prophecy will always be consistent with Scripture, will always edify, exhort, or comfort (the first two are not always comfortable), will always glorify Christ, and in the case of predictive prophecy for which any necessary conditions have been met, it will **always** come to pass.

Thus we must understand that prophecy, because it can have such great influence on the decisions people make in their lives, is not something to be taken lightly, to be guessed at, or to be left untested and free from scrutiny. If you're are in any way uncertain about a prophecy, it's best to keep it to yourself, or to share it only with mature leaders capable of judging such matters. This may seem overly cautious, but in truth herein is the 'secret' to 100% prophetic accuracy. It's not rocket science, it's just a matter of keeping your mouth shut until and unless God has revealed something to you. Once you are certain, it's time to apply the next key.

A Prayer for Certainty

Father, forgive me for every time I spoken in your name without being sure, and help me to recognize your voice in all seasons.

2
A DIVINE MANDATE FOR DISCLOSURE

But the prophet, which shall presume to speak a word in my name, which I have not commanded him to speak, or that shall speak in the name of other gods, even that prophet shall die. (Deuteronomy 18:20)

The last eight verses 18th chapter of Deuteronomy present us not only with a messianic prophecy, but also with a paradigm for the character and function of the New Testament prophet. Here we are shown that at that time, if a prophet were to bring forth a **definite** word from God, but God had not expressly commanded him to speak it, the penalty was death. This should cause us to consider the gravity of speaking a word in God's name.

When I've taught on the prophetic and this particular passage comes up, someone nearly always feels compelled to say something to the effect of, "But this is the New Testament! We're under grace." My response is usually, "Tell that to Annanias and Sapphira." God killed two people, in the New Testament era, for lying about an offering. Now, am I saying that God will always kill someone for prophetic presumption? No, but we shouldn't see God's mercy as his approval.

The underlying premise of genuine prophecy is that God has not only revealed something, but also that He has expressly directed the prophet (or other person) to disclose what He has revealed. Indeed, the very definition of prophecy in a scripturally sound context is divine communication. Absent of a divine mandate for disclosure, prophetic revelation is inevitably subjected to self-will, which is **never** an acceptable substitute for the leading of the Holy Spirit.

When I lived in Texas, I knew a prophetess who believed that it was entirely up to her to decide whether she should disclose something God had revealed to her. She'd said, "It's my gift, it's subject to me." She then went on to try to justify her position by citing 1 Corinthians, which says "the spirit of the prophets is subject to the prophets." However, this interpretation of that particular verse is a grave error. Let's take a look at that verse in its context:

> Let the prophets speak two or three, and let the other judge. If any thing be revealed to another who sits by, let the first hold his peace. For ye may all prophesy one by one, that all may learn, and all may be comforted. And the spirits of the prophets are subject to the prophets. For God is not the author of confusion, but of peace, as in all churches of the saints. (1 Corinthians 14:29-33)

Now, when we see this verse in its context, what we ought to notice first is that this was never about whether a prophet has the 'right' to decide to withhold a prophetic word, but it was in fact instruction given by the apostle Paul concerning the congregation's need to take turns when prophesying so that there would be order in the church. It never says that the gift is subject, but rather that the prophet's own spirit is subject to him. Nevertheless we must also consider any passage of the Bible in relation to the entirety of Scripture. Thus when we consider this phrase in light of Deuteronomy's definitive statement that the prophet is to disclose prophecy according to God's express direction, we can only conclude that this passage could not by any stretch of the imagination be telling us the exact opposite. God is not schizophrenic!

Therefore, the only circumstances in which we ought not to disclose a prophetic revelation is when we are uncertain of its content, unsure of whom it is meant for, or of when to release it, or when God has directed us not to disclose it. Why then are so many prophetic leaders teaching God's people that it's up to the prophet to decide whether a word is to be disclosed?

There's a fair number of answers for this, but ultimately it comes down to the motives of many leaders. One of the unfortunate truths of contemporary ministry is that many otherwise good and caring leaders often adopt the teachings and practices of more prominent leaders without questioning their validity. Largely this happens because they are seeking to imitate the success of leaders they see as role models, but in so doing they are following a work of the flesh referred to as emulation (Galatians 5:20). This isn't a condemnation, but rather an observation, and a call to those leaders to repent of violating their own divine mandate in favor of imitating others. In other cases, they go along with this practice for the same underlying reason their more prominent counterparts promote it: self interest.

By teaching that it's up to the prophet to determine whether a prophetic revelation is to be disclosed, the prophet can then insulate himself from genuine accountability by picking and choosing what prophecies he will share. How does this represent self interest? There are numerous ministries which will now offer to seek the Lord on your behalf in exchange for a fee. Some go so far as to refuse to deliver the prophetic word unless you pay their required 'seed.' Most of these ministries will perform theological acrobatics to justify this practice, but there is no justification for it.

While it is true that in ancient times when people went to a prophet to inquire of the Lord, they often brought a gift for the man of God, such gifts were considered a courtesy and were not required. We will deal with this issue in more detail in Chapter 6, but for now let us consider the fact that prophets in the Bible routinely refused gifts, and there is no Biblical record of **any** prophet in right standing with God requiring a gift to deliver the word of the Lord. After all, if God commanded you to speak, how dare you refuse to obey him unless someone pays you to do so?

It is good to be a blessing to a prophet, but the prophet ought not to demand a gift as a condition for the release of the Word of the Lord. It's the Word of the LORD, not the word of you or me. It's not ours to withhold or to sell.

Prophecy must always be disclosed EXACTLY as God gave it to you.

The divine mandate for disclosure isn't just a good idea, it's necessary. Imagine for a moment that you went to a neurologist, and he told you that he'd like to operate on your brain, and that it's a very risky operation but that he's not sure if it's there's a real need for it. How eager would you be to lie down on the operating table? I use this example in particular because in many cases, prophecy performs a function very much like surgery on the hearts and minds of God's people. It may very well happen that you will have to deliver a word to someone who's been horrifically abused and needs to be restored, and because of the emotional and psychological defenses they've put up, anything other than **exactly** what God told you to say will only make matters worse.

Many years ago, in a church my parents attended when I was a toddler, someone was moving in the prophetic and delivered a word that silenced the whole church. They said, "The Lord says that there is someone here with a homosexual spirit. Come forth, tonight is your night. The Lord is going to set you free." One of the men of the church came forth, head bowed. Before anyone could pray for him, an elder of the church who favored this young man as a up and coming preacher took the microphone and said, "What the Lord wants to say is that Brother X has a beautiful ministry, and he doesn't want the enemy to ruin it."

Years later, as the pastor of a church in another state, Brother X was caught in his church office with another man. He could have been free so long ago, but the presumption of one person changed the atmosphere and stroked Brother X's ego just enough to turn him away from the repentance that would have facilitated his deliverance. This is a tragic example, and it is my hope that it will exhort you to take care in how you deliver the word of the Lord. Always remember that someone's long-term deliverance or bondage just might be in your mouth!

A Prayer for Clarity in Disclosure

Father, forgive me for any time in which I've presumed to speak in your name, and grant me the wisdom and understanding to know when you are directing me to share what you have revealed to me. Reveal to me every habit of thought, conduct, and speech that may have contributed to presumption on my part. I surrender my gift to your leading, and thank you for committing this gift to me.

3
DISCLOSURE MUST BE MADE TO THE APPROPRIATE PARTIES

Surely the Lord God will do nothing, but he reveals his secret unto his servants the prophets. (Amos 3:7)

Some things are meant to be a secret, and God isn't going to trust you with too many secrets if you don't know how to keep one. This is perhaps another issue which should be obvious, but the unfortunate reality of contemporary prophetic ministry is that many prophets just don't exercise a level of discretion consistent with the gift and the office. Some might say they ought not to be blamed, as they've been taught incorrectly. However, to a great extent this is as much a matter of common sense as it is one of prophetic integrity and discretion.

Open rebuke is better than secret love. Faithful are the wounds of a friend; but the kisses of an enemy are deceitful. (Proverbs 27:5-6)

At times it may very well be necessary to correct and rebuke people, and sometimes openly, but such correction had better be undertaken because of a clear divine mandate. It occurs too often that some prophets become enamored with rebuke because of the power it gives them over people. One prophet I knew walked up to someone then commented that she looked scared. He laughed, and then said, "I love it!" After a very brief moment in which he looked as though he'd told on himself, he said, "You gotta love what you do," as though this justified what he just did.

Now this may perhaps seem to have little to do with the matter of disclosure to the correct parties, but this obvious pleasure that the prophet got from rebuking people led to some very unfortunate incidents in which he humiliated people unnecessarily. In one case, when a bishop who'd come as a guest speaker had been really well-received by the congregation, this prophet shared with them some details of the bishop's marital life that would have best been reserved for private intercession. In time this tendency eroded the congregation's trust in him as a leader. As I tell my business clients, trust is a precious commodity, and nearly impossible to regain once it's betrayed.

When I was younger in the Lord, I'd belonged to a church where the prophet had people so scared that he would tell the whole congregation their personal business that when he announced that a very prominent prophet, would be coming to the church. He said that she was really bold and had no problem embarrassing people. I'll admit that I was worried, because I didn't have skeletons in the closet. The bodies were still warm!

However, she did nothing of the sort, and I almost didn't go to those services. Over the next several years this prophetess proved to be instrumental in my own development in the kingdom. Yet the perception created by the pastor had very nearly robbed me of a blessing.

There was a young prophet who served on a worship team, and though he was earnest and well-behaved, the rest of the team just didn't like him. They were fairly mean to him at times, and would even try to tell him that his spirit 'wasn't right,' and other such things. He knew, however, that there was sin in the camp, and this was the underlying reason for their attitude toward him. One day, he became so frustrated with what was going on, he said to one member that they ought not to be giving him such a hard time when there were lesbians on the worship team.

As you might imagine, it didn't take long for this to get to the pastor, and this young prophet was called into the pastor's office. The pastor said to him, "I hear you said there were lesbians on the praise and worship team, and I believe you're right. But you can't tell everything you see. Just because you see it, doesn't mean you gotta say it. We trying to build around here." While the pastor's motive in saying this was that he wanted his church to grow numerically, and he wasn't about to upset the apple cart by making some very gifted singers sit down, there was a measure of truth in his words. There are some things that God will reveal to you that just aren't meant for public consumption. Some prophetic knowledge is intended for fasting and prayer, or for disclosure only to those with the maturity and authority to pray concerning those things.

It also frequently happens that a prophetic message is intended specifically and exclusively for one individual or a particular group, yet many prophets have developed the habit of sharing everything the see and hear in the spirit with everyone who'll listen. This ought not to be so. Now, everything isn't meant to be a secret, and there are many things which can be disclosed widely without causing harm, but it is paramount that the prophet not develop the habit of telling it all to everyone. When you have this habit, sooner or later, you **will** let something slip, and when you do, you will have to answer to God for the damage you cause in doing so.

Thus those of us who minister in the prophetic would do well to be sure not only of whom a particular word is for, but also whether it is to be disclosed in the presence of others, and who else is permitted to receive such disclosure. Not everyone who seems to be mature is mature, and just because someone **is** mature in the faith, it doesn't necessarily follow that God intended for them to receive a particular prophetic disclosure.

The solution to this issue is in the end simple. Pursue a close walk with God, so that you not only perceive what your gift enables you to, but that you also perceive God's will for just how to administer the operation of the gift.

A Prayer for Direction in Prophetic Disclosure

Father, please forgive me for every time I've presumed to share what you've revealed to me with people for whom it was not intended. Help me to discern correctly whom I should share your revelation with, and help me to be silent when I should.

4
DISCLOSURE MUST BE MADE WHEN GOD DIRECTS

To every thing there is a season, and a time to every purpose under the heaven. (Ecclesiastes 3:1)

There is indeed a set time for **every** purpose under the heaven. This is no different for prophetic disclosure. Imagine for a moment that a prophet were to warn you about a potential car accident two days after you'd already broken your back in a crash. God forbid! That would hardly be helpful.

It isn't so much that the prophet must always disclose prophecy immediately, or even quickly. Patience is not the ability to wait a long time, but it is rather the ability to wait until the appointed time. Many prophets fall into error in this area, and most often it brings us back to the issue of motives. The prophetic is often seen as exciting and glamorous. It's also not a secret that if you become known for frequent and accurate prophecy (or at least exciting prophecy), you're likely to be in demand as a guest speaker. You're also more likely to have opportunities to preach at larger, and consequently, more financially profitable venues.

This may seem to be a jaded view of the world of ministry, but it's a truthful view. It is, regrettably enough, true that many pastors have long since realized that a prophet who prophesies often can be a powerful ally in raising offerings, and the growing number of prophets who are quick to set up 'prophecy lines' according to the size of people's offerings firmly attests to gain as one of the major motives.

For others, the eagerness to prophesy is rooted in insecurity and what I like to call Triple-A Pride. They're often looking for attention, approval and admiration, and they can get all three if they just prophesy. This often leads to prophetic words being released prematurely, words being delivered to the wrong people, and in some prophets being taken over by a spirit of divination.

I knew of a young prophet who'd found that when he didn't prophesy, the offerings were smaller, and he was less likely to be invited back to preach. He also enjoyed the attention he received as the Prophet of God. Thus, when the Lord didn't use him in prophecy, he would become depressed and discouraged. It was not long before he was infested by a spirit of divination, and soon he was prophesying often again. The Lord had allowed this spirit to take him over because his true desire was not to serve God or his people, but rather to serve his pocket and his ego. Now, some might say that God would never allow such a thing because it would endanger his people, but I will have to tell you today that God can let you choose your doom while protecting his people from you. In fact, there are cases in which God will execute judgment among his people through corrupt prophets. In 1 Kings 22, this is precisely what happens. God sends a lying spirit upon the prophets of Ahab to ensure that he will go to his death.

The call of God on your life, and the precious people He has purposed for you to minister to are far too important to for you allow such motives to lead you astray. If you have even the slightest iota of this motive in your heart, I beseech you by the mercies of God to put this book down, turn down your plate and repent in sackcloth and ashes.

It's obvious to most of us why it's wrong to deliver a prophetic word too late, but very often we don't realize the full danger of a premature prophetic disclosure. As mentioned before, in Deuteronomy 18:20, we are shown that the prophet who spoke a **real** word in God's name without being expressly commanded by the Lord to do so was to be put to death!

This might seem a harsh punishment indeed, but let's consider why a premature word can be so dangerous. When I was in my mid-twenties, I belonged to a group of men who met for prayer early in the morning, and the leader of that group became one of my first mentors in prophetic ministry. One day he said something to me that I'll never forget. "Brother Sam," he said, "A word from God given prematurely is even worse than a word from the devil." I raised my eyebrows in disbelief at first, but as he expounded on what he'd said, I came to understand that he was right. A real word from God that's given before its proper time will often still witness in the listener's spirit, and they will perceive it to be a genuine word from the Lord. However, they may not always perceive that the word is for a set time and not something to be acted upon immediately.

The usual result of such a thing is that the person receiving the prophecy will jump the gun and act upon what was prophesied, not knowing that they are functioning outside of the will of God. Often this will happen partly because they were more eager for the promise of God than for His will. In Hebrews 10:35 we are told that we receive the promise **after** we have done the will of God. However, since prophecy often contains information about outcomes or potential outcomes, our human tendency is to pursue the outcome without embracing or even perceiving the process necessary to it.

Why does God allow such things to occur? I won't pretend to have a complete answer for this, since there are far too many circumstances to cover in just one chapter of a book on prophecy. However, I can say that it does appear in some cases that God will allow us to experience such situations and the potential shipwreck of our faith, not to test us, but rather to present us with a mirror in which we can see just how misguided we've been, and that where we thought we'd been acting in faith, we'd really just been acting in presumption. There are also cases in which it appears that the individual who was given prophecy in such a manner is being used as an instrument of judgment in the life of the presumptuous or careless prophet. God will preserve that person through the difficulty arising from acting on a premature prophecy, but woe unto the prophet whose words caused one of God's little ones to stumble! (Matthew 9:42)

Even when the receiver of prophecy fails to discern that the word was given prematurely, this does not absolve the prophet of his role in the matter. Carelessness and a cavalier attitude toward the consequences of the prophetic word we deliver and how we deliver them can have disastrous consequences for the people we've been called to minister to. The soul at stake could be your own.

The timing of a prophetic disclosure is as important as its content. Just as a heart surgeon shouldn't begin his work until the blood flow is bypassed and the aortic clamp is in place, we who operate in the prophetic must not merely be accurate, we must be precise. This is not a difficult thing to accomplish. Indeed, it becomes easy if we simply learn to completely rely upon the Holy Spirit's guidance.

A Prayer for Correct Prophetic Timing

Father, forgive me for every time I did not wait on your precise timing to release prophecy. Cleanse my heart and mind from motives that are not from you, and give me a wise and understanding heart to know when you are directing me to release your prophetic word.

5
ORDER AND AUTHORITY

For rebellion is as the sin of witchcraft, and stubbornness is as iniquity and idolatry. Because you have rejected the word of the Lord, he has also rejected you from being king. (1 Samuel 15:23)

The most commonly referenced passage of Scripture concerning authority is Romans 13, but we'll start with this passage because it deals with the very channel of the prophet's authority: the word of the Lord. This passage of scripture is often used to persuade people to obey what a prophet is saying. However let us consider it in terms of how the prophet's authority is intended to function. The prophet would be unwise indeed to expect to have authority when he himself does not submit to authority of the written word of the Lord, which has set forth the order of the household of faith. Thus we should first deal with the need for submission to authority in general before dealing with the matter of submission in prophetic protocol.

If indeed authority comes from God (Romans 13:1), then the prophet must see to it that he is submitted. How can we dare to claim that we speak the oracles of God when we are disobeying him? Indeed, our submission serves not only the purpose of obedience, but it is necessary to the integrity of our testimony in the world at large. I once knew a prophet who said he was "held to a higher law," and he apparently thought that this meant the laws of the world did not apply to him. No matter what car he drove, he drove it like he stole it. He ran red lights, performed illegal u-turns, and in general riding in a car with him was not for the faint of heart. I'm not sure who taught him this foolishness, but I will say that the prophet, and anyone else serving in a leadership capacity in the body of Christ ought to be even more diligent to see that they abide with the laws of the land, so long as those laws do not contradict God's word.

This being said, rightful submission to authority is an absolutely essential component of prophetic protocol, for a wide number of reasons. The prophet who cannot submit to authority cannot submit to God.

Rebellion is equivalent to witchcraft in the sight of God.

It is impossible to please God while disregarding authority. Indeed even our prayer becomes abomination when we rebel against God (Proverbs 28:9).

We see in part (1 Corinthians 13:9).

You may have received a genuine revelation from God, but you may not have the whole picture. It could well be that God has already spoken to the authority in the house, and the word you felt necessary to openly declare may have been meant for a private disclosure to the leadership. Nonetheless, if God does expressly instruct you to disclose prophecy, then disclose it you must.

Submission to authorities delegated by God is a vital part of becoming conditioned to obey God.

Even Jesus learned obedience (Hebrews 5:8) and no disciple is above his master (Luke 6:40). Godly submission is part of this process. The time I spent cleaning the church became times of prayer, worship, and intercession during which I received a great deal of revelation, and during which I grew in the Lord. There may be times when you will be assigned to seemingly unimportant duties which will help to shape your character and to teach you about the kingdom.

Your submission is part of your testimony.

As stated elsewhere in this book, people may not read the Bible, but they will read **you**. Is your conduct and character a living epistle, or a live performance of *Jekyll and Hyde*?

You cannot receive a mantle that you will not submit to.

During my twenties, the Lord showed me that submission causes you to be entitled to the full benefit of the anointing of those in authority, **even if they never walk in it themselves**. If only the prophets of the Lord would fully grasp this principle! Remember that Saul had the anointing of the King of Israel, but he never was able to complete the conquest of the Promised Land. David kept his submission, even through Saul's persecution, and it was under his reign that the territory of the kingdom was fully established.

Submission, or the lack thereof has a direct impact on your prophetic perception.

Many of us who serve in ministry are familiar with the 23rd Psalm, which says, "You anoint my head with oil," (v. 5) and most often we think of this in terms of the empowerment of the Holy Spirit. This is valid, but there is yet further revelation to be had. Shepherds of that time would smear the heads of their sheep with oil to protect them from vermin. If the sheep struggled to much with the shepherd, or even bit him, it was possible that it would not get a complete covering of oil, and it would become susceptible to vermin that could lay eggs in its ears or nose. The eventual consequences of this were that the sheep would have difficulty smelling clean water, detecting the presence of predators, and hearing the voice of the shepherd clearly. Likewise, when we rebel against the authorities God has placed in our lives, we can become susceptible to infestation by spiritual vermin, and our very ability to clearly perceive what God is revealing to us can become hindered as a result.

Rebellion in a prophet is profoundly dangerous.

I have known many prophets over the years, and I have been training prophets and other ministry leaders since 1998, so I've had more than a few opportunities to see rebellion at work in a prophet. Now, remember that rebellion is equal to the sin of witchcraft (1 Samuel 15:23). The prophet I mentioned before who had the dangerous driving habits also had issues of prophetic presumption. He began to believe that if he said something, God was somehow obligated to fulfill it, and many of the dreams and visions he had which he felt were prophetic were simply nonsense. He soon returned to a lifestyle of sexual immorality, and the kingdom lost a potentially very powerful prophet as a result.

Years ago, when I frequented a certain prophetic chat room on the internet, I encountered a number of prophets, the most memorable of whom was at times **very** badly behaved. He would come into the chat room and greet everyone by saying, "HEY YOU GOATS!" I'll admit hat at the time I found this funny, especially since there was usually more than one goat in the room. This prophet did, however, possess startling accuracy, and at one point even warned me about a matter in my personal life. His word came to pass, and spared me from a considerable amount of heartache.

However, this mischievous prophet had other rebellious tendencies, and his behavior became progressively worse. After some time, he disappeared from that chat room. Some time afterward, we met in person with another prophet we'd encountered in the same chat room, who we'll call Jake. He had a tragic story to tell us. Jake had known the misbehaving prophet personally, and had even housed him during a time when he'd been in need. The bad prophet had been using his gift to gain the confidence of vulnerable women. He would then seduce them, and take their money. Jake had been given a frightening word for this prophet, that if he did not cease from what he was doing, the Lord would kill him.

He came to live with Jake, and for a while, he seemed to reform. It wasn't long, though, before Jake discovered that the troubled prophet had a growing interest in pornography, and as time progressed, his interests in that industry became more and more vile. By the time he departed from Jake's home, he'd begun watching child pornography. Neither myself nor Jake have heard from this prophet since.

Some of you may wonder why God would allow one of his prophets to fall so far from the grace to which he'd been called. The truth of the matter is that when we persist in rebelling, there can come a point in time in which God will leave us to our own devices. Remember that in Romans chapter 1 we are told that:

> Because they did not see fit to acknowledge God, God gave them over to a debased mind and to do things that should not be done. (Romans 1:28 RSV)

It grieves me to think of this prophet, who could have been of great use to the kingdom. Now, not every case of a rebellious prophet will come to such a tragic state, but this story should cause us all to examine our ways.

Respect the House.

When the prophet must function in a place over which someone else is in authority, he must be sure to respect the house. Remember that your purpose as the prophet is to bring restoration, clarity of purpose, and divine direction. This does not mean that God has appointed you to place of authority over the leadership of that house. There are some instances in which a prophet must minister in a situation in which he or she does have greater authority within the kingdom, but even this does not mean that the prophet should run rough-shod over the set order of the house.

In the navy, an Admiral who comes aboard a ship will not take over command of the vessel unless it becomes **necessary**, and even then, he can only do so because he is expressly authorized to do so at his discretion. However, within the kingdom of God, the discretion concerning command decisions always rests with the Holy Spirit. It's never up to our own opinions, no matter how right they may seem to be. God sent you to help, not to take over!

Having said all that, we must also recognize that there is a difference between authority and tyranny. Yes, pastors, as the overseers of the congregation, the prophet must submit to your authority in the house, However, this is balanced by the fact that you must not use your authority as a means of controlling events and circumstances to suit your own self-will.

More than a decade ago, I was listening to the radio program of a certain leader I knew, and people were calling in with questions. One clearly prophetic woman began to tell him how the Lord had begun using her in prophecy and deliverance, and that she'd been ministering to people in various places, and there had been many testimonies of people being set free by the grace of God. The leader at first rejoiced with her that such a thing was occurring, but the tone of the entire show changed when she asked him a question. Her pastor had told her to stop casting demons out of people, and to stop ministering to them, and she wanted to know what she ought to do. The leader's answer was that she should submit to her pastor and cease at once.

> And John answered and said, 'Master, we saw one casting out devils in your name, and we forbade him, because he follows not with us. And Jesus said unto him, 'Forbid him not: for he that is not against us is for us.' (Luke 9:49-50)

There is no scriptural basis of authority by which a pastor or other church leader can rightfully forbid someone from casting out demons. Now, I'll have to qualify that by saying that I'm speaking of individuals who are **genuinely** expelling unclean spirits, and not people who are trying to, or who think they are ministering deliverance but aren't. The ministry of deliverance is exceptionally dangerous for someone who is not duly prepared to engage in it. We should **never** presume to minister in any capacity without the express direction of the Lord.

In the particular case I've mentioned above, I perceived in the Spirit that this woman had really been casting out demons and ministering in the word of the Lord. So, why then would the prominent leader on the radio program tell her to go along with what her pastor had said? I'd like to say that he was being cautious, or trying to respect that pastor's authority, but I know better. Another sad truth of contemporary ministry is that those who promote the idea of the pastor's authority being absolute will have more doors open to them to minister. Many pastors suffer from insecurity, jealousy, and a need to control, and so few pastors will invite you to preach in their church if they think you might upset the apple cart they've taken so much care to arrange.

Yes, there may be cases in which a pastor will prevent certain people from ministering for good and valid reasons, including the need to protect his flock from unsavory influences and tainted doctrine. I wholeheartedly commend those men and women of God who remain vigilant for the souls entrusted to their care. At the same time, we as leaders must also be certain that our protective zeal isn't a mask for other motives.

With these things said, we can now attend to the matter of specific protocol for conducting prophetic ministry within a setting that is overseen by an authority, such as a local church body. The issues we've discussed in previous chapters cover the principal matters, but they do bear repeating, at least in brief.

There must be certainty of revelation.

There must be a divine mandate for disclosure.

Disclosure must be made to the appropriate parties.

Disclosure must be made when God directs.

In addition to these things, I'd like to share with you some things I've learned about exercising the prophetic under authority. First, I'd advise you to find out how the leadership approaches prophecy, and adjust accordingly, unless it violates scripture, and unless God has given you express direction to do otherwise. This having been said, these are the rules I adhere to when prophesying within a congregational context.

Exercise your gift in order.

When possible (if it's a large gathering) have a microphone available for use in the event that someone has prophetic message. It's also wise to have water on hand for the person prophesying in the event that their throat gets dry during a long prophecy, as well as handkerchiefs or towels for sweat, as some people perspire heavily when ministering.

The person who believes they must share a word from God should check with whoever is presiding over the gathering, unless they've been given liberty to do so already. There are a number of churches in which the leaders have told me that I am free to share the word of the Lord whenever the Lord directs me, and I don't take this trust lightly.

Lay hands on no man –or woman– suddenly.

The Bible tells us not to lay hands on anyone suddenly (1 Timothy 5:22), and while this is an admonition about appointing leaders, it also applies to the practical matters of the prophetic. Do not rush to give prophetic liberty to untested and unseasoned people. Also, don't be quick to physically lay hands on people while ministering, either. Wait on the direction of the Lord. Also, be mindful of what is appropriate. When praying for women, I either lay a hand on their head, or I ask my wife to lay hands on them. I do this because I've seen some very obvious and shameful displays of lust by people in ministry insofar as just **how** they laid hands on people. I'll spare you the details. If you don't have a spouse who can lay hands on people of the opposite sex, you can keep to the head or hands, or just keep your hands to yourself, and no one will ever be able to accuse you of touching them inappropriately.

Never interrupt the service for a personal word unless God has expressly directed you to do so.

Let the prophets speak two or three, and let the other judge. **If any thing be revealed to another that who sits nearby, let the first hold his peace.** For ye may all prophesy one by one, that all may learn, and all may be comforted. And the spirits of the prophets are subject to the prophets. For God is not the author of confusion, but of peace, as in all churches of the saints. (1 Corinthians 13:29-33)

If there is more than one person with a prophetic word, don't interrupt one another. Speaking out of turn doesn't stop being rude just because God spoke to you. If you have a genuine word from the Lord, then represent him in your manners as well as in the message itself. Once the word is given, the prophecy should be judged. We'll discuss this in detail in the next chapter.

How to bring forth a prophetic word during worship.

I've found that it is advisable for church leaders to establish among their elders, worship leaders, and prophetic individuals some kind of non-verbal signal to let the leadership know that someone has a prophecy. Whatever procedure you may implement, it's best that it be discreet, swift, and orderly. Having some manner of signal or procedure in place will help maintain order and it will also make it easier for the service to follow the Holy Spirit's leading. Too many churches miss out on the full benefit of prophetic ministry because they are so rigid in their service format that they are unable to change directions when God does.

Speak clearly. Take your time, and speak at a pace that other will understand. If you experience 'stage fright' there is a very simple solution. Get over yourself. Nervousness and fear in public speaking occurs because we are being self-conscious, which is a nice way of saying that we're thinking of ourselves. Remember that it's not about you. It's about God and his people. Focus on that, and you'll find the idea of speaking before an audience less daunting.

If the trumpet give an uncertain sound, who shall prepare himself to the battle? (1 Corinthians 14:8)

Take a deep breath, slow down, and just deliver the message. When you're done, return the microphone to whomever handed it to you (if there is one), go sit down, and be grateful that the Lord chose to use you to speak to his people. Don't add your opinion, interpretation, or that sermon you've been birthing for the last six months. According to 1 Corinthians 14:29, it's not your job to interpret or judge the prophecy. If you are asked to clarify something about it, **and** you have been given understanding of it by the Lord, then do so. Otherwise, just be the messenger and then sit down.

Exercise restraint.

Not everything that God will tell you, show you or cause you to know is intended to be openly or publicly disclosed. Sometimes a prophet will be so excited that God spoke to him that it never occurs to him to determine whether God intended the revelation to be shared with others. There are things the Lord revealed to me over the years that I've never told anyone, because I understood that they were meant only to be prayed about, or because the Lord had made it clear that I was not to talk about them. In one particular case, someone knew that I'd been praying about some family members of theirs, and this person wanted to know whether the Lord had said anything to me about the situation. When I told this individual that I felt what I'd seen was not to be disclosed, she asked me to pray and ask God whether I could tell her. I did, and the answer was "Under no circumstances." It's likely that I'll take what the Lord showed me to my grave.

Never feel obligated to produce a prophetic answer for every question that comes your way.

You aren't God, and He never intended for you to have all the answers. It's good and right to pray for people, and to seek the Lord on their behalf. However, there are many cases in which God is not going to tell you anything, simply because he wants that person to seek Him for themselves.

Do not allow others to pressure you to prophesy.

You're God's prophet, not theirs. Also, bear in mind that using your gift according to self-will is in itself rebellion. Many prophets have entertained spirits of divination because of being more eager to prophesy than they were to serve the Lord. They who are led by the Spirit of God are the sons of God, not they who are led by their own opinion, or that of others, and it is sometimes the duty of the prophet to remain silent.

Exercise discretion with prophecy that is very personal.

There will be times when God will reveal things to you about people that are so personal that a public disclosure could be embarrassing or even humiliating. Unless God has expressly told you to speak it openly, you'd best turn the microphone off and whisper it to the person. I once knew a prophet who openly addressed a couple's marital problems, and to this day I remember the horrified look on their faces. They never returned to that church.

Is it possible that God instructed the prophet to deal with it openly? Perhaps, but considering the nature of the problems they were having, I doubt it. In my experience, it is very rare for God to direct the prophet to publicly disclose things which are of a sensitive nature. However, when there has been persistent stubbornness in refusing to turn from sin, God can and will embarrass you. Indeed, in a passage in which Paul instructs Timothy concerning dealing with leadership, he directs him to rebuke sinning leaders openly (1 Timothy 5:20). This brings us to another sensitive point of protocol.

How do you administer prophetic correction to leaders? Is it even appropriate to do so?

A lot of leaders will not like the answer. However, let me first say that if you feel led to correct a leader you had better be absolutely certain that God is directing you to do so. Unfortunately, there are too many prophets who will claim to have heard from God just to give themselves 'permission' to tell a leader off. This is unseemly, and ought not to be done.

Rebuke not an elder, but entreat him as a father; and the younger men as brethren. (1 Timothy 5:1)

If a leader is to be corrected, the first thing we ought to consider is this command. Now, while it applies to elders in age, it can also be applied to our elders in the Lord. While in the case of flagrant sin an open rebuke might be appropriate, unless I have a specific command from the Lord, I will entreat rather than rebuke, and privately. All this having been said, it is very rare indeed for God to direct someone to publicly rebuke a leader, and rarer still for someone to be commanded by God to rebuke someone whose leadership they serve under.

Now, I am not in anyway encouraging anyone to go running half-cocked presuming to correct your leaders. It is first required that if an accusation is to be brought against an elder, that there ought to be two or three witnesses present. This is not only for the sake of order. There may be times when someone you've corrected will attempt to twist what you've said, and when that happens having witnesses may very well protect your testimony.

In the vast majority of cases, when God has revealed to you a fault, flaw, or failing in your leader, the purpose of such revelation is for you to intercede on their behalf. At the same, time, leaders, you must understand that God can and will use people under your authority to correct you from time to time. One of the many dangerous teachings we tend to cling to as leaders is that only someone of higher authority has the right to correct us, and by believing this we very often become persistent in things which God wants to change in us.

Indeed, if when someone you believe to be to 'low' in rank to correct you does happen to correct you and your reaction is something along the lines of, "It's not your place to say that to me," the real issue is that you're proud and you don't want to change. No matter who you are in ministry, never reject the truth because you think its bearer isn't what you would consider an equal in rank. According to the word of God, I am in authority over my wife, yet

God has used her many times to show me that I was wrong about something. Since some might argue that a wife has a relationship with a husband that a congregation does not, let's take a look at a Biblical example of a leader being corrected by someone under their authority.

> And the Lord sent Nathan unto David. And he came unto him, and said unto him, There were two men in one city; the one rich, and the other poor. The rich man had exceeding many flocks and herds: But the poor man had nothing, save one little ewe lamb, which he had bought and nourished up: and it grew up together with him, and with his children; it did eat of his own meat, and drank of his own cup, and lay in his bosom, and was unto him as a daughter. And there came a traveler unto the rich man, and he spared to take of his own flock and of his own herd, to dress for the wayfaring man that was come unto him; but took the poor man's lamb, and dressed it for the man that was come to him. **And David's anger was greatly kindled against the man; and he said to Nathan, As the Lord lives, the man that hath done this thing shall surely die: And he shall restore the lamb fourfold, because he did this thing, and because he had no pity.** And Nathan said to David, Thou art the man. (2 Samuel 12:1-7)

Nathan the prophet was an Israelite, and as such, prophet or not, he was a subject of the king. Yet he rebuked the king for what he had done concerning Uriah. However, let us also note that he was never disrespectful. Thus if we must deliver prophetic correction to a leader, we had better do so tact, dignity, and respect.

What should you do when the leadership refuses to let you prophesy?

I've heard quite a few prophets complain that they had a prophetic word but the leadership of this or that church didn't believe them, or refused to let them deliver it for some reason or other, or with no reason given at all. There are perhaps some questions you might want to ask yourself if this ever happens to you.

Was this word meant for disclosure?

Did God **tell me** to share this word with the group?

Was this the right **time** to share it?

In some cases, it may well be that the prophet didn't hear a real word from God, and the pastor rightly stopped him from delivering it to the people. In other cases, the word itself is legitimate, but it was either not meant for public disclosure, or the time was not right for it to be disclosed. Now, the leader may not be aware of either of the latter specifically. He may very well just have a sense that the word shouldn't be released. When this happens, it's best not to resent it, but rather to respect the leader's decision.

However, it does at times happen that a prophet receives a genuine word of the Lord, and it **is** meant to be disclosed, and to be disclosed at that particular time, but the leader forbids it. Sometimes the leader simply didn't recognize it as a genuine word .This happens more often than we as leaders like to admit. It may also occur that the pastor or other leader forbade you because of unrighteous motives. In either case, it is best that you conduct yourself with grace and dignity, and follow the leading of the Holy Spirit. Now, most people who teach on the prophetic will tell you to simply accept the leader's decision and sit down, because God is testing whether you have the maturity to submit to authority. There may be some cases in which God is teaching you submission, but to give this line of reasoning as the blanket answer for all occasions simply isn't truthful.

Shall we have truth in the inward parts, prophets of God? (Psalm 51:6). There are times in which a leader may forbid a prophet to speak, but the prophet has been commanded by God to do so, and he must obey God before men (Acts 5:29). There will be times when a prophet **must** deliver a word, whether a leader wants him to or not. However, be forewarned: this is **ONLY** if and when GOD has specifically and expressly COMMANDED the prophet to do so.

You've been warned.

How to receive a prophet.

There's quite a body of material on this subject, and much of it is, regrettably, based on the self-interest of the prophets. From prophets who require a specific sum of money just to show up, to the one who will get back on the plane if the car which comes to pick her up isn't worth at least $150,000, prophets in the last few decades have done a great deal of dishonor to the office by demanding honors unnecessary for the execution of their duties.

One even went as far as to develop the habit of only responding when addressed as "O Exalted Prophetess." While we ought to treat all of God's ministers, great and small, with respect, this sort of shenanigans is just foolishness. Don't tolerate it. Now, I am aware that some congregational leaders **will** tolerate all manner of rude, arrogant and demanding behavior from prophets who are effective in raising large offerings, but I call heaven and earth to witness between us, that God has called you to walk above such behavior.

How then, do we truly honor a prophet of the Lord? When I was younger, the pastor of one church use to say, "The Bible says when you give to a prophet, you receive a prophet's reward." Indeed, this notion has been used very effectively by people in prophetic ministry to manipulate people into giving them money, but that is **not** what the Bible says. Let's take a look at what it **really** says and examine just what it means.

He who receives a prophet because he is a prophet shall receive a prophet's reward, and he who receives a righteous man because he is a righteous man shall receive a righteous man's reward. (Matthew 10:41)

This never says that one must give the prophet anything to receive a prophet's reward. While it is right and good to be a blessing to a prophet who serves faithfully, this passage is not about simply giving the prophet money. It speaks of how the prophet is **received**. This speaks to how we welcome the prophet, how we treat him, and ultimately, how we respond to him as the prophet of God. If the prophet truthfully tells you that God is calling you to plant churches and you hand him a check for $10,000 and go onto a long career as a doctor, did you really receive him as God's messenger?

> And Samuel said, 'Has the Lord as great delight in burnt offerings and sacrifices, as in obeying the voice of the Lord? Behold, to obey is better than sacrifice, and to hearken than the fat of rams. ' (1 Samuel 15:22)

We have truly received the prophet of God when we have obeyed God's voice. If we hear the word of the Lord, and bless the prophet financially, but have no intention of obeying God, then God has no delight in our offering. Indeed, doing so is wicked, and the sacrifice of the wicked is abomination to God (Proverbs 15:8). Now, to this I must add a word of caution. Beware any prophet whose prophecies are about people needing to give him money. Can God direct a prophet to raise an offering? Yes, but consider how rare it was for a Biblical prophet to ask anyone for anything. Yes, the Bible says that we will prosper if we believe God's prophets, but the prophet who uses 2 Chronicles 20:20 to entice you to give is hardly credible. Use your discernment.

These things having been said, there are some practical suggestions I would like to submit for your prayerful consideration with regard to how to treat the prophets among you. Treat them with love and respect, and be a blessing to them when you are led by God to do so. When it comes to prophets who are coming to minister to a group, there are a few things we ought to do so that the prophet is unhindered in the execution of his office.

Where possible, set aside some private space for the prophet to seek God. It is also preferable not to discuss what's been going on at the church, or share any details which might cause him to have opinions that could interfere with what he hears from God. Even when well-meant, this can easily lead to the prophet being biased in his ministering. Remember, even Elijah and the great Biblical prophets were just 'men of like passions.' (James 5:17) The prophet is only human, so please use wisdom in your conversations prior to ministry going forth.

If the prophet has any **reasonable** requests regarding accommodation, food, and soon, comply with them when possible. Use whatever godly means are within your reach to see that the prophet is comfortable, and bless him as you are able. At the same time, prophets, remember that though Paul taught that the ministers of the Lord have the right to reap of the carnal things, he also expressed that he did not exercise this privilege for the sake of the Gospel. Likewise, we serve in prophetic ministry do have a right to have our needs seen to, and even to be blessed by those to him we minister, we should also follow the example set by Paul and do what we can not to be a burden to God's people.

In my own ministering, I make no demands, but simply request a quiet place to pray, a comfortable and quiet place to sleep (if staying overnight), and water to drink while ministering. If they decide to do above and beyond that, I'm grateful, but I first make sure that they can bear the expense without harm. Seek to be a blessing, and trust in the Lord to bless you for it.

For the full benefit of prophetic ministry to be experienced, there must be order in both how such ministry is delivered, in how the prophet is dealt with, and with regard to the authority under which his ministering occurs. Let us commit ourselves to godly order so that both the prophet and those to whom he ministers can be blessed beyond measure.

A Prayer for Rightful Prophetic Order

Father, forgive me for every way in which I've exercised my gift in a manner not consistent with your divine order. I ask you to cleanse my heart and mind of every wrong assumption, every tradition, and every wrong attitude I've had concerning authority, prophecy, and your kingdom, so that I may rightly perceive your direction and follow it faithfully.

6
WALK WORTHY OF THE GIFT AND OFFICE

And the LORD spoke to Moses, saying, Take the rod, and gather you the assembly together, you, and Aaron your brother, and speak you to the rock before their eyes; and it shall give forth his water, and you shall bring forth to them water out of the rock: so you shall give the congregation and their beasts drink. And Moses took the rod from before the LORD, as he commanded him. And Moses and Aaron gathered the congregation together before the rock, and he said to them, Hear now, you rebels; must we fetch you water out of this rock? And Moses lifted up his hand, and with his rod he smote the rock twice: and the water came out abundantly, and the congregation drank, and their beasts also. And the LORD spoke to Moses and Aaron, Because you believed me not, to sanctify me in the eyes of the children of Israel, therefore you shall not bring this congregation into the land which I have given them. (Numbers 20:7-12)

Leave your opinion out of it.

In today's prophetic ministry, there's enough confusion regarding whether a prophecy was true. Still further confusion occurs when prophets presume to speak their own opinion when ministering, and by doing so they misrepresent God. This was the sin Moses and Aaron committed. After having led the children of Israel out of Egypt with great signs and wonders, Moses was now forbidden to enter the Promised Land, and Aaron had to die for his role in this incident.

While God doesn't always kill people for presumption, certainty of revelation is an absolute necessity. Moses and Aaron could have given the children of Israel the impression that God was upset with them. Now, in Numbers 14, the people had complained to such a degree that God sentenced an entire generation, minus Joshua and Caleb, to die in the wilderness. However, this time, God had simply instructed Moses and Aaron to speak to the rock, and he would provide water for his people. Because the water flowed, the children of Israel could easily have assumed that God had told Moses to speak to them in the way that he did.

Now, Moses had good reason to be upset and frustrated with the nation he was leading. However, even an opinion which seems to be correct has no place in prophetic discourse. One thing the prophet must always be mindful of is that the perception that he represents God can often cause his words to be taken as being prophetic, even when they are not. For new and immature believers this is particularly dangerous, because it can cause them to develop a distorted perception of God and his disposition toward them. It's probably best to be silent if you can't exercise the discipline to keep your opinions to yourself.

Many of today's prophets will often add their own opinion to a genuine prophetic word, which is equally dangerous. Remember that the Word tells us, "A little leaven leavens the whole lump." (Galatians 5:9). Much in the way a small amount of yeast will make a whole loaf of bread rise, even a small amount of opinion can distort the entire meaning of a prophecy. Always remember that we as people misunderstand one another often enough as it is. The word of the Lord does not need your opinion or mine to complete its work.

> And he said, Hear now my words: If there be a prophet among you, I the Lord will make myself known unto him in a vision, *and* will speak unto him in a dream. My servant Moses *is* not so, who *is* faithful in all mine house. With him will I speak mouth to mouth, even apparently, and not in dark speeches; and the similitude of the Lord shall he behold: wherefore then were ye not afraid to speak against my servant Moses? (Numbers 12:6-8)

While this passage of scripture is most often used to teach about authority, there is further revelation to be had if we look just a bit closer. Aaron and Miriam felt as though they had a legitimate complaint concerning Moses having taken a foreign wife, and sought to validate this complaint with their status as prophets of the Lord. This is a particularly insidious sin of presumption, because in attempting to validate an opinion with our prophetic office we are in fact making the claim that God has agreed with us, which may not be the case (and often isn't).

This practice is has unfortunately been encouraged in some circles, because people who don't readily follow a leader's good examples, will follow a bad example in a heartbeat. Thus, I have encountered many prophets who to attempt to validate all manner of opinions by stating that they are a prophet. I've known still others will assume that anything they say must be inspired, and sometimes go so far as to say 'God said.' Now, some of you are probably thinking "That's lying!" The truth is **every** deliberate attempt to superimpose the mantle of the prophetic on our opinions is a lie. The lives and ministries of such individuals are always marked by chaos, confusion and strife.

Now, the involvement of opinion doesn't always happen for nefarious reasons. Very often a well-meaning prophet will hear from God, or see a vision, and in his zeal to share what he's heard, what he will do is share his interpretation of the prophetic message, not the message itself. For example, there are many prophets who will pray for someone and see a house, and then assume that this is a house that God is going to bless that person with. As stated in the first chapter, if you're not absolutely clear, take it before God until it is. Even then, until you become adept at recognizing the voice of God, it's best to let the message be tested by mature prophets unless God has directed you to keep it to yourself.

Stay humble.

I've known too many conceited prophets, and this is something we who are leaders in the church must deal with. How can we dare to claim to be moving by the Spirit of God when we do not display its fruit? A prophet who lacks humility will often lack other elements of the fruit of the spirit, and will be highly susceptible to demonic suggestion in his ministering.

Watch your motives... and your mouth.

When a prophetic revelation is disclosed improperly, the underlying cause is nearly always a lack of discipline, or an issue of motives. When we allow our opinions to become involved, it's usually because our motives aren't right. One thing I've noticed over the years is that the prophetic plus opinion easily turns into gossip. Once this happens, you're not a prophet, you're a talebearer.

> You shall not go up and down as a talebearer among your people: neither shall you stand against the blood of your neighbor; I am the LORD. (Leviticus 19:16)

There was an express command not to engage in gossip under the Law. Now, many Christians today believe that the New Testament does not require obedience, but in Romans chapter 8 we are told that the work of Christ and the Holy Spirit are to establish the righteousness of the Law in us (Romans 8:4). Furthermore, we are reminded in 1 Thessalonians 4:11 and 2 Thessalonians 3:11-12 to mind our own business.

As mentioned in Chapter 2, there must be a divine mandate for the disclosure of prophetic revelation (Deuteronomy 18:20). Disclosure which occurs outside those parameters due to carelessness is dangerous, but when it happens because of unrighteous motives, it is abomination.

> The sacrifice of the wicked is an abomination to the Lord; how much more so when he brings it with a wicked mind? (Proverbs 21:27)

I've known many prophets, and one of the most shameful tendencies among them is one of using what they know as a prophet to intimidate and bully those around him. Years ago, I was teaching at a church, and a young man asked a question. Before I could answer him, the pastor of that church weighed in on the matter, but the young man disagreed with him. The pastor was soon frustrated by the young man's ensuing questions, and he began to berate him with details of his personal life in an attempt to humiliate him into silence. The young man looked hurt, but then said, "Well, I just came to hear Brother Sam," and then left. The pastor's real motive had been to assert his dominance, because he didn't want to 'lose face" in what was becoming a heated argument. However, he just came across as a bully. Unfortunately, this shameful display was far from being an isolated incident, and it was this issue of character which ultimately led to that church closing its doors as people left.

There may be times when as a prophet you will have to correct and rebuke people, but take care that you do so at the Holy Spirit's direction. Your stewardship of the revelation you receive from God is a privilege and a responsibility, and the integrity of that stewardship will determine just how much more God will trust you with.

Watch your temper.

I also knew a pastor who had a bit of a temper, and was often frustrated with his congregation's seeming unwillingness to follow his vision. The truth was that his authoritarian, bullying style of leadership made people reluctant to fully trust him as a leader, and some of his expectations just weren't reasonable. Whenever he was particularly frustrated, he would speak very harshly to the people, and he often referred to this as PMS – Prophetic Mood Swings. In one of these 'mood swings,' he went so far as to throw down his microphone, denting its outer metal screen. The congregation had just bought this rather expensive microphone for him, which was probably why the mid-week offering wasn't quite what he'd expected it to be. To this day I wonder whether it ever occurred to him that it was not only rather unseemly to throw such a tantrum, but it also made him seem ungrateful.

Now, he may not have realized it, but more than a few people in that church knew that these foul moods were not in any way prophetic. He was just upset, and still had some issues of maturity and self-control to work out. Nevertheless, the sin of presumption involved here was dangerous indeed. To a less mature believer, it would have seemed that God was volatile, easily angered, and hard to please. The truth, however, was that the prophet needed to realize that the real reason he was so often frustrated in attempting to execute his vision was that he was too often led by opinion rather than by divine mandate, and that intimidation is far less effective in leadership than inspiration. Unfortunately, no one would tell him that what he was doing was wrong, because most of the congregation was intimidated by him, and he wouldn't have listened to them anyway.

Yes, we were created to have emotions. However, we were never meant to be controlled by our emotions. Especially for those of us who serve in any leadership capacity, it is imperative that we not allow a bad mood to work its way into our ministering. Indeed, if you have mood swings of any sort, you would do well to seek out the root of the matter – and deliverance if necessary.

Be mindful of your testimony.

In my consulting business, I teach my clients about what I call behavioral branding. In business, it's crucial to one's vision to build a brand, and in both business and ministry it's inevitable that you **will** build a brand. Some, like Dr. Steven Henkel will say that behavioral branding is the idea that the employees of a company are the best ambassadors of its brand. I agree with this assertion, and I believe it also applies the the effect that our conduct and character has on people's perception of us, our ministry, and God.

People may not read the Bible much, or even at all, but they **will** read **YOU**. Despite the fact that many people in the prophetic ministry try to act mysterious, and even downright spooky, the truth is you're not as mysterious as you think you are. Almost no one ever is. Most of our behavior is quite transparent. Therefore, as representatives of God, his kingdom, his Gospel, and his people, it behooves us to behave ourselves in a manner that will give people no just cause to speak ill of us and of the Lord.

When David murdered Uriah to conceal his adulterous affair, the prophet Nathan told him that he'd given the enemies of the Lord opportunity to blaspheme (2 Samuel 12:14). When people blaspheme on their own, that's their sin. When they blaspheme because you've misrepresented God and his kingdom, it's **yours**. How are you 'branding' the kingdom?

Another often-disregarded aspect of our testimony is our relationships. In 1st Peter, we are told to treat our spouses with honor, so that our payers will not be hindered. If you won't exercise proper care and affection for your spouse, and therefore are hindered in your prayer life, how can you possibly hear from God clearly and consistently? The answer is that you can't. The same applies to our various other relationships in life.

The prophetic ministry is often a ministry of dealing with people, and while we have to please God before men, we will not please God while we're mistreating his people. Never forget that Moses was denied entry into the Promised Land because of just **one** incident in which he spoke harshly to God's people without need. One of the great truths of the kingdom is that no one gets to the Promised Land alone. I've seen too many ministries fail and close down because the leader mistreated people who were necessary to the vision and they left. Yes, God can and will replace rebellious people who leave, but it often happens that he does not replace people you've mistreated.

Now, there are some prophets who may seem to go on to great things even while treating people horribly. While this may seem like a contradiction, one thing I must warn you of is that sometimes God will judge you by giving you exactly what you wanted. I have known a number of people who seem to have been blessed by God after doing all manner of wrong to others and never repenting for what they did. Some of them have even gone so far as to act as if they were somehow the victims! Yet the truth of the matter is that God has allowed some of these people to seemingly get what they want in order to ensure that they will never repent for what they've done.

Some of you will believe this to be too harsh. Some might even say that God is a loving God and would never do such a thing, but we are told otherwise by Scripture. In 2 Thessalonians 2 we find that God is perfectly capable of sending someone a strong delusion to cause them to believe a lie in order that they would be condemned because they did not believe the truth but delighted in wickedness (v. 11,12). Be mindful of how you deal with others!

Our stewardship over the basic matters of life is also an important aspect of our testimony. One popular motivational speaker often tells his audience, "How you do anything is how you do everything." While this isn't necessarily precise, there's a great deal of truth to it. After all, Luke 16:10 tells us:

If you are faithful in little things, you will be faithful in large ones. But if you are dishonest in little things, you won't be honest with greater responsibilities.

When I applied for my first mortgage, the broker said something to me that will stay with me for the rest of my life. He told me that he was surprised to find out that I was a minister, but not because of my conduct or speech, but rather because I had good credit. He went on to tell me that in the mortgage industry it's well-known that preachers are usually hard to create mortgages for, because they often have bad credit. This ought not to be the case. While misfortunes can happen to us all, very often the real cause is a failure to be responsible. Whether it's your credit, a messy car, or your table manners, the stewardship you exercise over your life is in most cases an indicator of underlying character issues that can and will find their way into your ministry.

Some of you may feel that these issues aren't part of protocol, but the truth is that how you live your life **will** affect how you carry out your ministry. In Acts chapter 6, the apostles instructed the saints to select men who had a good reputation and who were full of the Holy Spirit and wisdom, just to serve food (v.3). If a good reputation, and being full of the Holy Spirit and wisdom is necessary to serve food, how much more important is our lifestyle to the ministering of the prophetic?

The testimony borne by your conduct and character will also have an impact on whether your ministering is received. When people reject the word of the Lord because they are being stubborn and rebellious in their sin, that's their problem, but when they reject it because the fruit of your character has tainted the credibility of your message, it's **your** problem.

Should the prophet require people to pay for prophecy?

In Chapter 2, we briefly mentioned the practice of prophets requiring a 'seed' in order to prophesy, and we will now deal with the various doctrinal arguments used to justify this practice. Now, some prophets will claim that they aren't selling prophecies, but that they are instead simply requiring that people sow a seed to support the ministry. This is at best self-deception, and at worst playing games with words to disguise the real motive, which is financial gain. No matter how it's worded, making a financial gift a prerequisite for the delivery of a prophetic word is selling prophecy. Some ministries have made millions of dollars doing this, from $37 personal prophecies online to the $1000 prophecy line at the local church.

As stated in Chapter 2, if God has given a prophet a specific word for a particular person, we have no right to withhold that message unless we are uncertain of whether God is directing us to release it. Now, there are a number of scriptural arguments made to justify this practice, and one of the most common is the ancient custom of bringing a gift to the man of God when asking him to inquire of the Lord.

Now there was a man of Benjamin, whose name was Kish, the son of Abiel, the son of Zeror, the son of Bechorath, the son of Aphiah, a Benjamite, a mighty man of power. And he had a son, whose name was Saul, a choice young man, and a goodly: and there was not among the children of Israel a goodlier person than he: from his shoulders and upward he was higher than any of the people. And the asses of Kish Saul's father were lost. And Kish said to Saul his son, Take now one of the servants with thee, and arise, go seek the asses.

And he passed through mount Ephraim, and passed through the land of Shalisha, but they found them not: then they passed through the land of Shalim, and there they were not: and he passed through the land of the Benjamites, but they found them not. And when they were come to the land of Zuph, Saul said to his servant that was with him, Come, and let us return; lest my father leave caring for the asses, and take thought for us. And he said unto him, Behold now, there is in this city a man of God, and he is an honourable man; all that he saith cometh surely to pass: now let us go thither; peradventure he can shew us our way that we should go. Then said Saul to his servant, But, behold, if we go, what shall we bring the man? for the bread is spent in our vessels, and there is not a present to bring to the man of God: what have we? And the servant answered Saul again, and said, Behold, I have here at hand the fourth part of a shekel of silver: that will I give to the man of God, to tell us our way. (1 Samuel 9:1-8)

First, we should note **why** Saul felt compelled to bring a present for the man of God. The term 'man of God' is only used in the Bible in reference to twelve individuals. We now throw this term around so lightly that we've forgotten how special it was meant to be. Then we must consider that Samuel was known to be an honorable man, and **everything** he said **surely** came to pass.

Something else we should note is the monetary value of the gift itself. A shekel of silver was $1/50^{th}$ of a mina, which was about 500 grams. So a shekel was about 10 grams, leaving Saul's servant with about 2.5 grams of silver, which at the time of this writing is worth about $1.89, hardly enough to get into the $1000 prophecy lines at some churches today. When they came to Samuel, the prophet gave Saul the seat of honor at the feast he'd prepared, and the best cut of the meat. It's good to honor the prophets of God. I encourage you to be a blessing to the prophets among you when you can, but considering how prophets in the Bible who were right with God made no demands of money or gifts, how do we dare to presume to do so? When you **deserve** honor, you don't need to demand it.

Another passage of Scripture frequently used to justify so-called 'prophetic seeds' is found in 1 Kings 17.

Arise, get thee to Zarephath, which belongeth to Zidon, and dwell there: behold, **I have commanded a widow woman there to sustain thee.** So he arose and went to Zarephath. And when he came to the gate of the city, behold, the widow woman was there gathering of sticks: and he called to her, and said, Fetch me, I pray thee, a little water in a vessel, that I may drink. And as she was going to fetch it, he called to her, and said, Bring me, I pray thee, a morsel of bread in thine hand. And she said, As the Lord thy God liveth, I have not a cake, but an handful of meal in a barrel, and a little oil in a cruse: and, behold, I am gathering two sticks, that I may go in and dress it for me and my son, that we may eat it, and die. And Elijah said unto her, Fear not; go and do as thou hast said: but make me thereof a little cake first, and bring it unto me, and after make for thee and for thy son. **For thus saith the Lord God of Israel, The barrel of meal shall not waste, neither shall the cruse of oil fail, until the day that the Lord sendeth rain upon the earth.** And she went and did according to the saying of Elijah: and she, and he, and her house, did eat many days. And the barrel of meal wasted not, neither did the cruse of oil fail, according to the word of the Lord, which he spake by Elijah. (1 Kings 17:9-16) [emphasis mine]

When this passage of scripture is used to entice people to give, rarely is any attention given to the fact that before Elijah even left the brook, God had already directly spoken to the widow, and commanded her to feed and house him. Then, when Elijah, tells her to make him a cake first, he prophesied to her **before** she gave him the cake. Now, this wasn't just any prophet, either. This was Elijah, whose word always came to pass. The same Elijah who could call down fire from heaven. Yet today we have prophets whose words fail often and yet they believe themselves to be entitled to honors that no Biblical prophet, not even our Blessed Savior himself, ever presumed to demand.

Now, consider this. As she went to bake that cake and used the last of her flour, she got to see the word of the Lord come to pass before she even fed the prophet. This is very different from the notion of demanding a 'seed' from someone in order to prophesy to them. Prophets, how many of you can guarantee that a miracle will happen **before** someone sows their seed into your ministry? Some will, of course, argue that sowing before the miracle takes 'greater faith,' or something along those lines, but the truth of the matter is that many prophets want people to sow a 'seed' for their request beforehand, because that way, whether your prayer is answered or not, they've still got your money.

I knew a church whose leaders had developed the habit of attaching an offering to prophetic ministry as if it were necessary. Prophecy would go forth, and perhaps some of it was even real prophecy. Then they would conclude the prophetic ministry by telling the audience that they had to "sow into the word" in order for it to come to pass. This is nothing but flagrant manipulation. Is it possible that God might direct someone to sow in faith? Yes, but in such cases, it is **never** right for the prophet to demand a 'seed,' or to manipulate anyone into feeling obligated to give. Remember, the Biblical prophets we were given as examples didn't do this. They didn't need to, because they trusted God to provide for them.

No, it's not wrong to collect an offering. It's good and right to give, and we should all do what we can to be a blessing to the true mend and women of God who are in our lives. However, if we use the prophetic to entice people to give, we become guilty of the same sin that Israel's prophets committed in Micah's time, and incur the same divine displeasure.

> The heads thereof judge for reward, and the priests thereof teach for hire, and the prophets thereof divine for money: yet will they lean upon the Lord, and say, Is not the Lord among us? none evil can come upon us. Therefore shall Zion for your sake be plowed as a field, and Jerusalem shall become heaps, and the mountain of the house as the high places of the forest. (Micah 3:11-12)

Jesus Christ, the prophet *par excellence*, told his first apostles, "Freely you have received, freely give." (Matthew 10:8) Now, he said this with specific reference to the work of the ministry, including the working of miracles. While ministry can come with costs and expenses, this is never an excuse to violate this simple and beautiful command. The real question, prophets of the Lord, is do you trust God enough not to rely on manipulation to provide for your ministry?

The prophetic ministry is not only needed in the church, it is necessary. Paul even exhorted the saints to desire to prophesy above all other spiritual gifts (1 Corinthians 14:1), because what God has to say is far more important, valuable, and useful than what any of us ever has to say. Knowing that the prophetic is a means whereby God communicates with people so precious to him that he gave his only begotten son for them, should we not seek to walk worthy of the great privilege of being the vessel by which his words are made known?

A prayer for restoration

Father, forgive me for every time and in every way I have not conducted myself in a manner worthy of the gift you have committed to me. Let my words, thoughts, and actions be acceptable in your sight, and teach me to represent you with grace, dignity, and holiness.

7
RECEIVING AND JUDGING PROPHECY

Let two or three prophets speak, and let the others pass judgment. (1 Corinthians 14:29 NASB)

One of the most insidious trends in the world of ministry has been the rise of a 'don't judge' culture, and it is particularly dangerous when it makes its way into prophetic ministry. Christ's admonition in Matthew 7:1 was made to a group of outwardly religious hypocrites who would condemn others while committing even worse sins. It was not an instruction to never judge at all. Indeed, in John 7:24 Jesus expressly tells us not to judge by mere appearances, but to judge righteously.

Thus it is, that when a prophetic message has been disclosed, judging the prophecy is not merely a suggestion, but a necessity.

Beloved, believe not every spirit, but try the spirits whether they are of God: because many false prophets are gone out into the world. Hereby know ye the Spirit of God: Every spirit that confesseth that Jesus Christ is come in the flesh is of God: And every spirit that confesseth not that Jesus Christ is come in the flesh is not of God: and this is that spirit of antichrist, whereof ye have heard that it should come; and even now already is it in the world. (1 John 4:1-3)

One of the things we ought to watch for before allowing anyone to minister in the prophetic is where they stand concerning this point. As the passage tells us, there are **many** false prophets, and it is becoming increasingly common that people in prophetic ministry no longer believe that Christ will physically return to establish his kingdom. They now teach that Christ has already returned in **them**.

Now, some of you may say that this passage talks about how Christ **came**, not how he's coming. What is interesting to note is that in the Greek, 'has come' is written in the perfect tense, which implies a past action with ongoing results in the future. In 1 Timothy 3:16 we see this idea expressed with the perfect participle *eleluthota*, which denotes a continued condition. Thus we must understand that not only did Christ originally come in the flesh, but he continues to have a physical, but eternally glorified body. In 2 John 7, we are told that

> For many deceivers are entered into the world, who confess not that Jesus Christ is **come in the flesh**. This is a deceiver and an antichrist. (2 John 7)

Here John used the present tense in the Greek which focuses specifically on the future coming of Christ. When considered with Acts 1:11, which expressly tells us that he will return in the same manner he left. This is stated within the context of a passage that also tells us that he showed the disciples with *infallible proof* that he was physically alive.

Thus we must understand that prophets who insist that Christ did not come in the flesh, or that he is not going to physically return have the spirit of antichrist, and it would be unwise to allow such a prophet to minister. It's one thing to have different views on some matters of Scripture, but it's another thing to hold a view which the Bible identifies as a definite indicator of having a spirit of antichrist. Such spirits never bring just one form of error. In my own experience, I have yet to meet a prophet who taught such things who did not also incorporate a good deal of New Age spiritualism and eastern mysticism into his teaching, preaching, and prophetic ministry.

When inviting a prophet to come minister to your congregation, it is also advisable to pray and investigate his character and testimony. Some of the most popular prophets in today's world of ministry have illegitimate children in multiple cities. While everyone's got a past, it's another matter entirely if the prophet has been committing fornication while in ministry. If he got three women pregnant in the last city he preached in, will the ladies in your church be safe from his sexual predations? Also, bear in mind that we can only impart what we have, and we cannot help but to impart what is in us. Would you pour your child a drink from a gallon pitcher of lemonade if someone had spat just a little bit in it? You'd probably be disgusted, and there's no way you're making your child drink from that contaminated source. Likewise, we must guard against contaminated prophets.

One of the most common contaminants in prophetic ministry is pride. Some prophets begin to become arrogant as their ministry grows, and this is never healthy for the prophetic discourse. In Deuteronomy 18, there is a messianic prophecy that also reveals the proper character of the New Testament prophet.

> The Lord thy God will raise up unto thee a Prophet from the midst of thee, of thy brethren, like unto me; unto him ye shall hearken. (Deuteronomy 18:15)

This tells us that the messiah would be like Moses, and so we must understand that the genuine New Testament prophet who is in right standing with God will also be like Moses in character.

Some will pose the argument that we're not all on the same level, so we can't all be like Jesus. Remember that the Bible tells us that the disciple is not above his master (Luke 6:40), and when it speaks of Christ being our example (e.g., 1 Peter 2:21) it uses the Greek word *huppogrammos*. This was a model alphabet given to a child on the first day of school so that he would learn to write. Christ and his character supposed to be the alphabet with which our life as believers is written. If you are going to minister to others, you ought to have at least the basic alphabet down!

We are told in Numbers chapter 12 that Moses was the most meek man on the face of the earth (v. 3). God does not raise up arrogant prophets, and as leaders we ought not to tolerate arrogant behavior. Remember the lemonade example.

> Every one that is proud in heart is an abomination to the Lord: though hand join in hand, he shall not be unpunished. (Proverbs 16:5)

Should we set an abomination before God's people to minister to them in any capacity? God forbid. Not only will he not escape punishment, but anyone cooperating with him will be punished as well. By allowing the proud prophet to minister among you, you set yourself under the judgment of God. In the financial world, there is a principle known as *due* diligence. It refers to the practice of thoroughly examining all pertinent facts before making an investment. Trust is an investment. Do your due diligence!

With all this said, the protocol for receiving prophecy can also be applied to judging prophecy. Now, we will all react in our own ways based on our temperament, character, personality, level of maturity, and circumstances, but there are still some things we ought to bear in mind when receiving what appears to be a word from the Lord.

First, be sure to have your own relationship with God. Too many people become 'prophecy junkies,' going from one prophetic gathering to the next in their quest to hear something from God. Prophecy was never meant to be a replacement for seeking God. Many of us want to hear from God through a prophet, while the Lord can and will speak to us through Scripture. For many people, the word they really need to hear is "Go read your Bible and pray."

Tongue-in-cheek statements aside, we must take care not to seek out prophets while having little or no relationship with the Lord ourselves. We are told in Hebrews 4:12 that the Word is a discerner of the thoughts and intents of the heart. We will be sorely lacking in discernment if we do not study the Word, and many people end up entertaining spirits of divination because they blindly seek out prophets almost as if dialing up the psychic network.

Don't read into it. Sometimes the receiver of prophecy, whether an individual or group, will read into a prophecy and misconstrue its meaning. The inevitable result of this that people will act on their perceived interpretation of the prophecy, and this tendency has cause a great deal of heartache for many believers.

Sometimes the circumstance, situation, or people that the prophecy pertains to has not yet come into your life, so be sure not to try to twist the prophetic word to fit your circumstances, or to fit a circumstance that you'd like to bring about.

Test prophecy against the Scripture. Knowing this, we must also test prophecy against the Word of God. Bear in mind that it's not enough to have a so-called 'proof text' as some have begun to call it. There are many false prophets in the world, and most of them are skilled in using a verse or two out of its context to justify almost any prophecy. In recent years examples have abounded of self-styled prophets who have taken portions of scripture and used them far out of their context to secure everything from monetary gifts to sexual favors. Therefore, we must pursue a life of diligent study of the word so as to have a good understanding of Scripture as a whole, so that we can rightly test prophecy against it.

Now, there are some prophets these days claiming that the Word of the Lord given to them has equal standing with, or even supersedes Scripture. This is a grave error, and you will find that prophets making such claim will **always** have prophetic revelations and teachings which will outright contradict Scripture. At best, these are immature prophets who've been taught this nonsense and go along with it because of unrighteous motives, and at worst, they are false prophets. In either case, they present a significant danger to the Body of Christ, and their ministering ought not to have a place in any church of sound teaching.

Edification, exhortation, and comfort.

Many of those who teach on the prophetic will insist that in the New Testament, all prophecy should be for edification, exhortation, and comfort (1 Corinthians 14:3), and it is most often assumed that all three of these characteristics should occur together, or that every prophecy must be soothing and comfortable. If this were true, then Christ himself would not have shared the prophecies in Matthew 24. Let us also consider the prophetic word in Acts 13:10-11, whereby a sorcerer was **struck blind**. Then there's the Book of Revelation, which contains quite a bit of prophecy which is decidedly uncomfortable.

When I served in the US Marine Corps, my drill instructors exhorted me often, and it was **never** comfortable, and yet they edified me in that I got into the best shape of my life, and developed habits of discipline which have proved to be very valuable to my spiritual life. I continue to to this day to be comforted when I encounter a dangerous or stressful situation and I'm able to deal with it calmly because of that training. When a skyscraper is to be built, ground must be cleared, any existing buildings must be demolished, and deep excavation must occur to secure the foundation. Likewise, the prophet must at times perform similar functions in order to build up the saints. Thus we must understand that while the end result of genuine prophecy is edification, exhortation, and comfort, some parts of this process may not be comfortable at all.

There should be an inner witness of the Holy Spirit. Now, there may be times when we receive a corrective word from the Lord, and our initial human reaction might be to believe it wasn't from God, since most of us don't like being told we're wrong. If a seemingly wrong or corrective word is presented, then the receiver of prophecy is best served by remaining calm and prayerfully considering what has been said. In my younger days, there were times when a prophet rebuked me openly, and I resented it, but in the end I had to admit that the prophet's word was right, and I needed to make some changes in my heart and life. Despite the initial emotional turmoil of embarrassment and resentment, once I inwardly admitted to the truth of the word given, I felt peace about it (Collossians 3:15).

Keep your composure and listen closely.

Some ministries now record prophetic words for later listening. This is a wise practice, and worth doing, both for the benefit of those receiving prophecy and for the purpose of keeping prophets accountable. However, many churches and other gatherings of believers do not do this, so it is important to maintain your composure no matter how the prophecy affects you emotionally. In this I speak primarily to people who 'lose it' when there's a prophetic word for them, and in their emotional outbursts or breakdown they fail to pay attention to the word being given.

Another reason to maintain one's composure is that there are many prophets who use the prophetic as a sort of performance, and when they see an intense emotional reaction, they will 'go with it' and may even embellish the prophecy just for the sake of making the experience more dramatic. Why would they do this? Yet another sad truth common in ministry today is that prophets whose ministering is dramatic and exciting tend to get invited back, and tend to command higher speaking fees. This doesn't mean they aren't prophets of the Lord, but it does mean that they have some issues of character and maturity to work out, and that leaders need to take care to put a stop to such performing.

Compare the word against what God has already spoken into your life.

Is it consistent with the vision God has given you for your life? Does it give direction to your purpose, or does it cause confusion? Now, there may be times when a genuine prophecy is not understood right away, which brings us to our next point.

Pray concerning the word.

Bring it before the Lord in prayer. Ask God to show you whether the word was true, whether it's for another season of your life, or if there are conditions you need to meet in order for it to make sense to you or come to pass. Ask him to confirm the word or refute it, in whole or in part.

Don't rush to act on it.

Too often people receive a predictive or directive word through a prophet and they immediately try to act on it without considering that the word may be for an appointed time (Habakkuk 2:3) which has not yet come. If it's a true word from the Lord, he will give confirmation if it is needed.

Bring the word before mature leaders in the Lord.

When a word seems questionable, or arouses discomfort, confusion or fear, share it with leaders who are seasoned in prophecy.

Seek God concerning the timing and conditions of the word.

If it is a true word from the Lord, begin to ask God what its timing is, and what you need to do to prepare for its appointed time. Too many people rush to try to make a prophecy come to pass, when the truth is that God isn't calling us to bring it to pass, but rather to align with his will so that we 'catch up' to that word at the proper time in the future.

Record the word in some way.

It is best to keep records of prophetic words so that those receiving prophecy don't have to rely on their memory, and it is also useful for accountability, but recorded prophecies are also valuable as a tool of exhortation when they come to pass. The record of the prophetic word becomes part of the testimony of what has happened, Remember the saints overcame Satan by the blood of the Lamb and the word of their testimony! (Revelation 12:11)

Once it has been determined that a prophetic word is in fact genuine and appropriately disclosed, then we enter the process of waiting for its fulfillment. However, waiting is not always a passive thing. Sometimes it will be necessary to pray concerning the word, and to begin implementing any strategies God revealed related to it, as well as seeing to the fulfillment of any prerequisites that might be involved.

This never means the we are to try to make a prophecy come true through our own efforts. Sarah did this, and to this day Hagar's children continue to cause trouble for Israel. Stand in faith concerning the genuine word of the Lord, and be led by the Spirit as you wait for its manifestation.

No matter how good the prophetic word might sound, and now matter how well-trusted the prophet is, we are commanded by the Word of God to judge prophecy. Thus in any gathering of the saints, at least one mature believer ought to be doing so. If we are diligent in how we receive and test prophetic disclosures, we will experience much greater clarity of vision and a better focus for our mandate in the earth.

A Prayer for Sharp Discernment

Father, forgive me for every time in which I have not rightly discerned prophecy, and for every time I have delivered prophecy in a manner that wasn't consistent with your will. Cleanse my heart that my motives would be pure, my discernment sharp, and my mouth a ready instrument for your glory.

ABOUT THE AUTHOR

Sam Medina is a best-selling author, award-winning artist, business strategy consultant, and Chairman of The Restoration Group, an apostolic ministry dedicated to the equipping and releasing of uncompromising Christians in every walk of life. A dynamic teacher of the Word, Sam has spoken at churches, universities, and business conferences throughout North America, and oversees a growing network of international ministries dedicated to the worldwide spread of the Gospel. He lives with his wife in the Toronto area.

You can connect with him online at

www.restorationgroup.org

www.sam-medina.com

and

@RIFT_CHURCH on Twitter

Made in the USA
Middletown, DE
25 February 2018